Public Speaking is Easier than you Think!

Public Speaking
is
Easier than you
Think!

By Charles Kos, PhD.

Plus Ultra Books

A Plus Ultra Book.

http://www.plusultrabooks.com.au
Melbourne, Australia.

First published by Plus Ultra Books, Melbourne, 2019.
1 3 5 7 9 KD 10 8 6 4 2

ISBN: 978-09874208-7-9 (paperback)

NATIONAL
LIBRARY
OF AUSTRALIA

A catalogue record for this
book is available from the
National Library of Australia

Typeset in *Helvetica Neue*.

This book is dedicated to you!

Acknowledgements

I wrote this book because I realised that there are very easy ways to becoming a good public speaker, rather quickly. These are not taught or very clear in the 'main stream.' I hope to share these with the reader.

I would like to thank my family for putting up with me while writing this!

Let's get to it

"HECK! I just can't do it! That's not me, I can't get in front of people like that?!"

So says a former friend of mine, in his fifties. He is convinced he cannot publicly speak. As such, he does not, and probably never will. But he wants to. For him speaking is overwhelming. This book breaks that down that myth and tries to make it easy, easier than you think!

This book is written in a kind of free-flowing style. There is a reason behind this!

We want to emphasise that the *style* you choose to employ in your speaking is **not** important.

You are not here nor expected to *ever* deliver a speech like Socrates before his final tribunal. When you are called up to make a dinner or wedding speech, you are never expected to be a Pericles delivering a funeral oration, or Abraham Lincoln, delivering the Gettysburg Address.

No-one speaks like that and you are not expected to… ever. In fact, once you begin to try to speak like those chaps, people will start to whisper that you must be… *insecure*!

Part of your work in becoming a good public speaker is realising perhaps what public speaking isn't. You have actually been public speaking your entire life. But it isn't an exam when strangers are present.

So how do you speak? AND, what is a speaker anyway? What does he talk about? I've discovered that the uncertainty about the answer to these questions, and particularly the last one, might just *drive almost all fear of public speaking*!

What does a speaker talk about?

The position of an audience and speaker is better explained as something like that of actor and audience, or even subject and interrogator. That's right, for your audience is your interrogator! For this reason, many novices become 'shaky and flakey' before an audience. Event the experts do! But *do not panic*, for this is the *easiest* interrogation in the world to pass!

In fact it's very easy to 'bluff' your interrogator and make the greatest speech in the world, even if you are not a speaker!

The audience will only ever expect you *to tell a story*, as if you were talking to your friends in the pub. Thats right! That's all it is!

But being in the position of interrogator, they want to see some fireworks. They want to see some action. In your speech you want a central

3

contention applicable to the lives of your audience. And, you want to keep going back to that contention throughout the speech!

So, formal or informal?

Between about the First World War and today, the formal 'dinner' speech began to be replaced, in a big way. Like dinner parties around a dining room table, it no longer exists.

In the past the formal speech was delivered by royalty or nobles, or those emulating them. Proud family members never ventured too closely to this, with exceptions.

Above all, it was a class-based type of speech delivered to impress people regarding the dignity of the occasion as well as the solemnity of the whole affair. It is now a lost part of our culture because of the eradication of class distinctions following the First and Second World Wars.

Thus, it is not in today's style. Just as beautifully-carved brown antique furniture has vanished, so has this style of speaking, which began to really disappear by the 1930s.

And yet when people hear about 'public speaking' they imagine this is what it is all about! Careful speech, crafted polished jokes (will they laugh?) and no slip ups! Sounds like a nightmare!

I have heard it said by Dutch people from the Netherlands, that the former-Dutch population, now located in Belgium (the Flemish), are 'insecure' because they 'talk like Shakespeare'. They, basically use a different, older form of Dutch.

Those Belgians seem to have a very round-about way of talking. They apparently use very long sentences, and their tone is allegedly theatrical.

This has negatives and positives. But, it certainly rubbed my Dutch friend up the wrong way. (Apologies to the Belgians)

You do not want to rub your audience up the wrong way. Simply confide (be confident) and be sincere, (literally, 'without care' as to the consequences). That is, be as honest as you can be, so long as you are avoiding the usual no-noes: sex/politics/religion, etc. You do not want any of that in your speech as someone is definitely going to cry.

The fact is, we want to communicate in the most *direct* way possible. A speech is communication, not poetry. (It can be) We want direct communication. If we take too long to say something, people will think: 'he is hiding something'!

So to pass your 'interrogation' when you begin to speak, simply be honest and sincere and tell a story which entertains *you*. Perhaps something which happened to you recently that was weird or fun?

Once I had an argument with my girlfriend. I was taking a long time to explain something, so she assumed that I must be 'guilty' and then criticised the lack of apology; actually I was trying to gently find out what was going on. The direct way is the better way when it comes to communicating.

In Holland, where I recently had a trip, many houses will refuse to have any curtains. They *want* strangers to look inside. Some like to show off their interiors. If you have curtains, it is again a case of: 'He is hiding something.'

When you speak, don't put curtains up. Pull them back.

It's a very controlled, observant society over there. The best way to communicate in such a place is to be observed, to be open; to be decent and act normal. This forces you to have a clean house, and clean, stylish front rooms.

In Holland, that's the best way to present yourself. AND, it's also the best way to present *yourself*, before an audience, when you develop your very own speaking style. Be normal, be a human being, be decent and be open, but make no excuses, for you are a leader. (The leader does not ask forgiveness while speaking.) I guess that is what they mean when they say: "Be yourself, be true to yourself."

Being direct and being yourself is very important indeed. Everyone has their own natural charisma which can be quickly brought to the fore. It is the aim of this book to do that, and quickly. I hope you enjoy it.

Toastmasters and Public Speaking: Opportunities to Begin.

I've long been a member of Toastmasters. This is an international speaking organisation which non-members sometimes compare to the Freemasons.

That is certainly more than a little bit of a stretch. I was a fan until they replaced magnificently-refined fifty-year old paper manuals with a very difficult-to-use online course which felt like it had been put together in a great hurry, and by outsiders.

Now instead of a social club, it feels like doing homework, the fun is gone.

For now, my club is allowing me to continue using paper manuals just to keep me along. Thank goodness, or I would be out of there!

They also reduced the quality of certificates you receive at each milestone, from a grand-old 19th-century style, flowing cursive-style certificate, to something cheap looking which you print out yourself. A bit sad and impersonal.

I do not see why they need to reduce the tone and caliber of the experience in this way, in 2019-20. But, I assume it is to save on 'overheads'. Maybe someone in toastmasters land is getting an enormous bonus for doing this.

If you were to pay to hear people speak, you would want this to be a pleasure, an enjoyment. This means that 'fun' is the name of the game, in any speaking environment. It means you should make your speech fun, and have fun while doing it!

We live busy lives and I find more people (including myself) are 'half asleep' most of the time, even though we seem to be fully awake. If someone is irritable or making flawed decisions, they may need way more sleep. This is partly why, I've found that *how* you deliver is more important than *what* you actually deliver, from an entertainment point of view.

While the toastmasters organisation goes south in my estimation, maybe the way of the dodo… opportunities for public speaking are growing exponentially. For years now, starting as a hobby and later as part of my vertically-integrated, Ancient-Mysteries publishing company, I've been making youtube videos. I pursue the ridiculous assertion that mankind's civilisation is hundreds of thousands of years old.

I started out showing a picture of a pyramid, and then a tunnel inside the pyramid and then the Sphinx. I started ranting and raving, it was my passion.

I filmed the screen and filmed my rants. People started subscribing. Soon thousands and thousands!

I put it down to being passionate. I was *interesting because I was interested.*

As soon as I became a roaring success, I noticed that I was suddenly a much better speaker, largely because I had found my authentic voice, my authentic self. It was conversational, interested, paced, with a bit of drama here and there.

People say I am 'unscripted' and 'spontaneous', even if I am actually reading from a script! I learned to add a spontaneity and flexibility to what I was reading. I mixed it up with pauses and went off on occasional short tangents. That meant, I guess, that I was 'unscripted'.

Balderdash.

"Don't read from Notes"

In toastmasters, everything is evaluated. If you try it out, don't be frightened. It just means that the same person every week is going to make the same comments on what you have to say.

Sometimes while being evaluated, someone will say: "Hey you read from notes… so… points **off** for that!"

You are allegedly "Supposed to memorise a speech."
Um… what?!

Firstly, what are these guys smoking?

It is physically impossible to 'memorise' a speech while you have work and other commitments. There is a reason toastmasters meets in the evenings after all! No-one is going to memorise a speech to be delivered only once, to ten people at toastmasters.

That's partly why I *always* use notes, and you should too! Do not even bother hiding them like cards in the palm of your hand. That's for amateurs!

Hold your notes high! Loud and Proud! I use notes on a pad of about A5 size. I find this about optimal. I write in big capital letters so I can always read my own writing.

My notes are basically dot points. Pointers to me of what to say next. I number each page with a big circle around each number. In this way the speech is planned in advance.

I used to make the mistake of delivering lecture presentations with powerpoint in the form of my dot points. Wrong. Powerpoint should be as simple as possible with pictures instead of text.

I find that a good, fun picture holds the audience' interest far better. The notes are your own alone. Do not cram lecture slides with them.

Speech-craft

In toastmasters if you are in a fantastic club, you have an opportunity to participate in something called 'speechcraft.' This is basically teaching public speaking to corporates and so forth who are paying the club for the privilege. I have been the M.C. of this several times.

I've seen literal miracles in this. People going from shy to incredible in only four sessions. Not everyone, but most improve incredibly.

Speechcraft is one of the best things I've ever done.

Phone around to different toastmasters clubs. By teaching public speaking, you can become an incredible public speaker. We *do* learn by teaching.

Our own Speaking Business

I've got a good friend called Nathan. We both want the same things in life. Get rich and become a solid public-speaking/motivational guru! Just like everyone else. Well, some other people. Well… ok… maybe just a few!

But in order to do this, we have to help a great deal of people, and that's what brings true satisfaction. We've both moved on from speechcraft and gone into business for ourselves.

While starting up, we realised that we could do things differently, improve a lot on what has been done. We have our own way of teaching which is unique and informative.

Your speech is actually a performance

Speaking is definitely performing. Before a speech, or before I MC ('master of ceremonies') a workshop, I will not eat anything for most of the day.

I want to have that raw, keen, hungry look and feeling about me. But, I will have about two coffees for energy. I will be overflowing with energy because I want that to rub off on the audience.

I tell our speaking customers that they need to supply 'energy' to their audience. This does not mean add sugar to the tea. It does not mean add *EXTRA* to the coffee. It means speak with energy and enthusiasm so that it rubs off.

The way to do this is to be entertaining… by yourself being entertained by your topic. The more neurons are active in your head, the more fun you are having.

The more of your brain is working, the more your muscles, which are connected to these neurons, tingle, and move around. An excited mind is an excited body. This is why listening to music helps one at the gym.

I tell people that so long as they are excited the audience is going to be excited.

So to be excited, talk about something that excites you. Stamp collecting is going to be a stretch, unless you really, really love it, and are able to communicate this love.

If you can do that, the people don't care what you speak about. You will usually be fun to watch!

So, *what* to talk about? I often suggest that people talk about something funny that happened to them while on their travel adventures.

Everyone loves travel (especially women). Women are gatherers (mainly) while men are hunters (mainly.) Women love to gather information and ideas all the time, which is why they love to travel indefinitely, to learn a particular landscape, and all about a particular place.

They see what grows where.

But in short, travel is a topic that everyone is usually crazy about.

Cooking is a great topic in the right hands! Talk about your misadventures in the kitchen. Talk about misadventures rather than adventures. Talk about love!

Talk about an awful restaurant experience. The audience will lap it up. They will enjoy the discomfort of the staff, the gruesomeness of the meal, the fly in the soup.

Talk about what turned you on the most, in life, and how it transformed you.

Test your speech topic against your own interest. What kind of speech would **you** physically travel to, to hear? Would you travel to a speech which lacked a message and failed to inspire? People usually travel to and pay for speaking events which are going to affect their lives in a good way.

What's your dream speech, that you want to listen to? A story of a dramatic rescue at sea? A fall from a cliff....? (Hey a literal cliffhanger!) Give your audience... *that speech*.

Authenticity and Sincerity

Authenticity is everything. It means you're being yourself. We want to know: "Who is this guy." We are always judging each other. That's why we all dress with the same latest fashions. Drive the same cars. Everyone competes with everyone else by looking like everyone else!

And while we are competing and judging, we are emphasising and trying to assess that person, and in fact judging everything about them. What kind of person are they? What is their sexual preference? What kind of hobbies do they have? We humans do this all the time!

15

Even more than authenticity is the quality of sincerity. I believe that next to enthusiasm, sincerity is the number-one value that you must have while talking.

Even better than sincerity is mixing sincerity with facts which are easy to grasp, for the persuasive speech.

Which speech is better: Number One?

"Hi everyone, I'm working for this big huge company. They are paying me thousands to rush around Australia talking. I love driving my BMW on the freeway but it gets boring having an expensive car believe it or not. Believe me, you don't want what I've got, because luxuries really get old.

I can count on my hand the celebrities who helped out our charity at the function last night but why embarrass them? They know who they are!

I'd love if you all donated to this great charity, I've donated thousands myself, hey you might help somebody else for a change! Did you know that this charity actually helps many many people?"

OR Number Two?

"Hi everyone. What would you do, right now, if you were poor and had nowhere to go? What would you do if you were about to be evicted from your home, through no fault of your own? How would you feel?

Let me tell you how many people we have helped with an example. How many of you have been to Sunshine? It's a suburb out west of Melbourne.

As you drive through the streets, it takes you about ten minutes to get from one end to the other. And that is quite a few houses. Who has driven through? [Wait for show of hands]. To put it into perspective, if we take all the places and families we have helped, we have helped about half of those houses in the past twenty years.

A family member of mine [true story btw] was evicted from her home. I only found about it twenty years later. She was too proud to let anybody know, too proud to ask for help. Even though we could have given that help a hundred times over, and readily and gladly, expecting nothing in return.

Naturally our whole family was mortified. We wished there would have been some way we

17

could have helped anonymously. But at the time there was not.

Some people are just too proud to ask. Maybe some of you or somebody you know. Maybe you will never find out. So one way to assist, is donating tonight. You might help that unknown person, by giving tonight, gladly, for the good of giving, and expecting nothing in return, but the feeling of making a difference, by being a true difference."

Obviously number two is probably a little bit better than number one. It has a powerful start, a good ending which wraps back around to the start. It has a fact which is tangible. It is also very sincere. Speech one is insincere and foppish. It comes from a position of under-command rather than command.

Five-minute dinner speech? How many points do you make? *ONE!*

In a three, five or ten minute speech, please do not bother to try to make too many points.

If you make *two* points, you're going to lose some of the audience. Not all, but some. If you make *three* points, half the audience will go to sleep. Do not bother with four points! We do not want to learn 'ten ways to fix your bicycle in five minutes.'

We instead want to learn 'one smart way to fix your bicycle if it breaks down and you haven't got any tools.'

Writing is the same. I try to stick to one point per sentence.

This doesn't always work and sentences do like to… grow.

I do wish authors would do this more often! Keep it simple if you want to reach the whole audience. This will help you to get a standing ovation from everybody, because you have not excluded anyone. You have kept it to the lowest common interest level.

The only way you can possibly do this is if you keep your speech to the lowest common interest level with one idea per speech. One idea per sentence… and a pause in between!

Keep wrapping around back to your central point, re-emphasising it in your conclusion. Easy!

Get rid of 'insecure' right now.

I met one a very rich man in his 70s. He was kinda 'insecure,' presumably the reason he had made so much money. I heard all this stuff I never asked about. His art collection, the fact he was on the board of football clubs, the fact he made a fortune in investment banking.

I don't like using the word insecure because it's demeaning and wrong. I mean before you are called insecure, check to see you have not actually been surrounded by robbers and bandits all your life!

Thus, people throw it around without knowing what it means. For example Kaiser Wilhelm II is described in TV documentaries as 'insecure', building a big army, latest technology. (If possibly starting World War One is insecure, please someone show me what secure actually means!) Heck the fact he lost proves he wasn't 'insecure' enough and should have built an even bigger army! His mistake was he was too secure!

In fact the most successful people were always the most insecure because if you're secure you basically don't need to get out of bed in the morning. Right?

Having said all that, this man was insecure on an interpersonal level. Or whatever you want to call it!
So how do you stop this behaviour? Surely no-one likes to hear this bragging during a speech?

Firstly others around us are never going to satisfy us totally, and are always going to disappoint us. So there is no point doing any bragging to these people. What you do is none of anyone's business.

We can get affirmation from within, not from others. It is one of the laws of 'confidence.'

Our audience really doesn't want to hear any bragging. It will turn an audience off. Being insecure will turn an audience away from you, unless you manifest that as your 'vulnerability factor,' which is truly your 'it factor' as a speaker.

Confide = be confident. Tell your audience things as if you were in a secret conspiracy with them. Tell them like you are a backslapping old friend. Let them know. Tell them some details. Whisper aside comments. That's being secure. Don't lecture them like a schoolmaster. They are your friends, your colleagues. Do you lecture those? Just talk like a human being. It's easy! We do it all the time!

Do not seek acceptance while speaking.

You have the power and the floor. You should be dressed well.

If having the Rolex makes you feel secure, or is your passion, heck, get the Rolex. Heck, I recently bought a 'gold' case for my phone to make myself feel better. Everyone is insecure.

But it merely means that we are incomplete, our lives still ongoing, and are not dead yet. Not that there is something wrong with us, so it can never ever be used to label someone in an absolute sense.

This is why I don't like calling people this. Some people are just tired, or 'tired of all the crap', more than others. No-one is fundamentally 'secure' or 'insecure'.

To get rid of 'insecure' and be very confident everywhere, simply realise that your affirmation comes from within, from being alive, being at the spring of the universal source. It will not come from others.

There is no need to rely on others or pander to them. If you are insulted, call them out, frequently if need be. They are not allowed to hit you, so be as 'rude' as you want. But never look for acceptance from other people. That's being rude to yourself. You will always be disappointed and 'insecure' if you try. And who wants to walk on eggshells?

How you convey, is better than what you have to say.

Dale Carnegie, the master-teacher of public speaking in the early 20th century wrote: 'When I see a man talk, I want to see him act as if he is fighting bees.'

In other words we do want some excitement. We want passion, enthusiasm. It lights us up. It is fun.

Be vulnerable!

Vulnerability rocks the audiences' world these days. It's the new 'it'. But even in the past, human nature has loved quotations which betrayed this confidence to us:

"I know not what others say of me, but I was always it seemed but a child walking on the beach, looking at shells.' So said Isaac Newton.

There is a proverb: "He who is exalted is humbled. He who is humble is exalted." Look no further than the biography of Jesus for evidence of this as recorded in the New Testament.

Look at the life of Ghandi, Mother Theresa. Look also to the fate of every dictator. How many can even have enjoyed a decent retirement? They can

23

never actually retire properly because they were never humble. They became objects of hate.

"I'm afraid of public speaking!"

You aren't. We're simply all afraid of what we haven't done before. We were afraid of bikes before we rode one. We were afraid of the water before we jumped in and soon became accustomed to it.

Everyone is always afraid of the unknown. The greatest-ever horror/fantasy writer, H.P Lovecraft said: 'Man's greatest fear is fear of the unknown.'

If you think that this isn't the case, consider the following passage from Arthur Conan Doyle's Sherlock Holmes story, *A Study in Scarlet*:

"… He expected that he would receive some message or remonstrance from Young as to his conduct, and he was not mistaken, though it came in an unlooked-for manner. Upon rising next morning he found, to his surprise, a small square of paper pinned on to the coverlet of his bed just over his chest. On it was printed, in bold straggling letters:—

"Twenty-nine days are given you for amendment, and then — —"

The dash was more fear-inspiring than any threat could have been. How this warning came into his room puzzled John Ferrier sorely, for his servants slept in an outhouse, and the doors and windows had all been secured. He crumpled the paper up and said nothing to his daughter, but the incident struck a chill into his heart. The twenty-nine days were evidently the balance of the month which Young had promised. What strength or courage could avail against an enemy armed with such mysterious powers? The hand which fastened that pin might have struck him to the heart, and he could never have known who had slain him."

In just the same way as John Ferrier was chilled to the bone by the unknowable, so is the first-timer to the art of public speaking. But this is simply because they do not know how easy it is. They do not know that it is just telling a funny story to your friends! And if your audience are strangers, treat them like your friends!

And so, you're possibly afraid of what you THINK public speaking is all about. Take all of what you think it is and throw that in the trashcan. Because it's none of that.

I don't want to come across as condescending, but if you are shy about public speaking, there is a gap. There is just possibly a gap between what you *think* is expected of you, and what actually is expected. That is to say, what a normal human being is actually capable of delivering.

You are never expected to be Superman when you are on stage. There is only one superman and that man is Christopher Reeve who is no longer with us.

I think, what people actually want is YOU. The authentic you. The real you. But just you…. and maybe a funny story. That's it! Tell a story. Even if it's about yourself. In fact… especially if it's about yourself. That's how you win at public speaking.

In one toastmasters set of meetings, over many months, I noticed a highly-narcissistic girl, was *slaying* every other speaker, repeatedly, always.

She won 'speaker of the night' whenever she got up to talk.
The speeches were always the same topic. Her and her vulnerabilities and insecurities. Hardly very informative at all.

They were literally filled with: '*I never thought I would be able to do this or that or I feel shy or vulnerable. English is not my language and I never thought I could…* etc…. I never thought I could speak in public… people always trying to put me down, but don't let anyone put you down, cos that's bad!.'

She delivered it all in a quiet voice and her tone was conversational. She never raised it for emphasis, never made any pauses, (you should use pauses to achieve a similar effect on your audience, to that achieved by the dreaded hyphen above!)

I never voted for what I considered to be 'this absolute tripe' because it was too much of 'me me me and screw the rest of humanity.' BUT, guess what? Others **LOVED IT!**

Their faces and expressions warmed up with tears in their eyes, as they began to recall feeling vulnerable themselves.

So, even though every other speech was always 'better', and with superior content, guess who always won? She owned that audience. Her speech was always the best speech.

I personally prefer speeches where I learn something completely new and informative, even if the tone of the speaker puts me or others to sleep. I mean that's the point of speaking, right? To deliver information?

WRONG! As it turns out! Mine is actually a minority viewpoint here! What most people actually vote for in contests is entertainment value. They *want* to be entertained, often by realising the amazing speaker before them is not their superior, but their equal... or even underling!

In one speech I heard, the guy was blathering on about travel. I was enthralled with the topic and loved it, but everyone was asleep. Did he win speaker of the night? Certainly not! The winner was a clown who technically delivered almost zero information. He was funny and he won.

'In the same vein', people will not vote for, or appreciate a 'preachy' type of speech. Maybe this is one reason why church attendance has fallen close to zero in the western world. Everyone it seems has a higher education and the priest is no longer the 'most-educated, wise person in the village'.

In this way, It is *really* a good idea to steer clear of being over serious. If you are a serious type of personality, simply try talking about a more funny topic. A funny topic delivered in a serious tone or by a serious or monotone-voiced personality is always utterly hilarious.

Such a speaker becomes very endearing indeed, and a favourite of their audience. If you are already a clown, the audience already loves you and talking about a clownish topic might be seen as a 'little too much.' Clowns, please consider a more serious topic!

How to deal with the 'talker' in the audience

Often, the interrupter or talker or commenter in the audience is jealous of the opportunity you have been provided, in your speaking, and just wants to be a part of it.

Fine. Usually you can humour them. Tell them that what they have raised is a 'pivotal point'. Flatter them a little.

I have heard criticism of Dale Carnegie's magnum opus: 'How to Win Friends and Influence People'. The criticism is basically that if you follow his strategy, you become a doormat for the wrong people because you flatter them too much with your attention.

That criticism is dead on. I think you become the most popular person when you don't become a doormat, and act like the very opposite to Dale's suggestions. Dale Carnegie tended to write things like: "You are the best ever conversationalist when you say little and let the other person talk."

In the real world, it's best not to be a people pleaser and to flatter no one except your superior at work, and your temperamental family members that you have to live with because you otherwise love them, or are actually being also genuine in your flattery.

So, we want to quickly silence the other person who is interrupting us, but without alienating the rest of the audience by being too abrupt. We should give them a little space but not too much.

I am not sure about you, but I would rather people walking on eggshells around me than vice versa. If the interrupter cannot stop talking due to possible autism, then it is time to harshen up, just a little.

Tell them 'OK! What you have to say is extremely important, but we are going to discuss it after.' Get to after….. after everyone else has gone home, if at all! Your audiences' time is your number one priority. Always. Always finish on time.

I've seen one book say that a polite insult might help. This is not suitable in workshops. It is more for the public or street arena when someone is being exceptionally rude. Something such as: "I didn't know they were giving out free booze', might be very well received, even by the person doing the heckling.

It's not about what you say but what you don't say

It is not about what you say but what you don't say that really matters, if you want to wow and hold the audience in your hand.

It's not about what you say to capture attention, because sometimes a pause in the right place is your best ally!

I put it to you that it's what you don't say..........
At all! .... that can capture an audiences............…... attention!

Speak with drama and the whole room is listening!

In the normal four week speech-craft course that toastmasters runs, or in the course run by myself and Nathan, we have both noticed some incredible things.

I would tell people in the second or sometimes the final or second-last class: "Look, you've all come here, with an agenda. You've tried to get up on stage, you've tried to be contrite and humble, looking at the floor, trying not to create too much of a fuss.

You've done that flawlessly, A+. So why not now, get up and be a champion, get up like you are a pro speaker. Put the image of a perfect pro-level speaker in your head and be that person.'

The change was beyond what I have words to say! Some of the members of the audience suddenly transformed into professional-level speakers, instantaneously. They were better than me! I told many of them, I'll have a talk to you after and get some pointers for myself. They became phenomenal.

I can only guess that these folks accessed some deeper level of their subconscious and brought it to the surface, for the subconscious is surely aware of every action in the universe that affects Earth, and a vast storehouse of secret information.

That is why it is not about *what* you say. It is what you *don't* say that holds the audience. You build the drama, you build theatrics, you suddenly become very *very* entertaining, as you tell your story.

Everyone is nervous, always.

I point out to students the experience of André Rieu. He is one of my roll models. He is the highest-paid musician in the world. He has about forty million dollars and lives in a 'Cinderella castle!'

He makes his performances seem to the audiences like they are attending the 'pumpkin-carriage ball'. There is enormous attention to detail and a personal touch, such as gifts handed out as wedding presents to couples beforehand, 'From Andre!'.

This makes so many feel feel utterly special. They become bowled over with excitement and surprise, as the cameras record it all for the cinemas and television.

For forty years he has been improving his 'Johann Strauss act' from, at first a regular orchestra, to a smiling orchestra with fantastic old instruments and fantastic theatrics and music. And they all wear eighteenth-century clothes of the fantastic old, aristocratic world, as it existed before the French Revolution.

Before an act, André struts down the stairs of his hotel in front of his adoring crowd. Cameras follow him all the way to the auditorium. Trumpets blast like at a royal wedding.

This is shown in cinemas worldwide. I was only able, so far, to see this in a cinema and let me tell you, the cinema audience actually cheered at the end!

He was asked in a recent interview: "So, after doing this for forty years, do you still get nervous?"

He said: "Yes, every time. You want everything to be perfect."

Please, don't let your nerves stop you doing something whether it is speaking or anything. Those nerves are your lifeblood. They mean you care.

I personally, before a workshop, feel very nervous! I pace around and look at my notes, sipping coffee to have more energy to give away to the audience. I love what I do, which is the only reason I do it. But I also want it to be perfect.

I don't really get nervous about the idea of speaking in front of a crowd, as that was conquered long ago. I only get nervous because I worry I may have forgotten to specify something important in my speech, or that everything needs to flow according to a certain timetable.

Being a historian, I used to run a walking-tour business as one of my first entrepreneurial ventures. I was speaking to crowds of forty or crowds of one. I was always nervous but it got a little better with time, once I knew exactly the kind of stories that turned people on.

But it took doing one tour about fifty times to really nail it, and I was always looking for some ways to improve. And believe me, you keep getting better and better, even after doing it a hundred times.

When you see a comedian on television or live and think: "Wow such talent!", be cautious. It's more likely evidence of practise and interest which I suppose in a way is talent.

What you do not see is them saying those same lines, that same act, a hundred thousand times, for all their life. So do not be nervous. If they were asked to suddenly get on stage, for the first time, they would be more nervous than yourself.

Your nerves are your excitement!

This is one of the best pieces of advice there is. Some people say: "turn that nervousness into excitement". Others feel they are very nervous and 'cannot possibly' get up there and talk because 'that's not them.' Rubbish!

Be the person that you are, on stage. It's simple! You never have to be like anyone else while speaking. People only expect you to be you. They only want you to be you.

I would refine the statement, 'turn that nervousness into excitement,' into…. 'those nerves ARE your excitement.' They literally are you being so excited that you finally have a chance to speak. You finally have a chance to express yourself!

Narcissism and what to talk about!

The most famous actors and speakers you see are all narcissists. This is fine. Everyone has a degree of self interest.
It's necessary for survival.

But these are not always people who have finished their mental or emotional development into adulthood. There are nice narcissists and there are bad ones.

We have all encountered the narcissist at the dinner table who will not shut up. This is the person who does not have the social skills to realise that it is rude to talk about themselves continually.

They do not understand that they hurt others who just want to have something to say, so they too can shine! To live, to speak, to breathe.

I encountered these people especially while I was running for a local municipal council… they were the other candidates! Unfortunately they never matured beyond say age two, while other parts of their head somehow managed to reach adulthood. Thus they become functional in adult society as if they were fully adult.

Or perhaps they were just crying out for attention. It is fascinating to listen to someone deliver a monologue all about themselves for ten minutes.

In my younger years I was shy and let this continue, still do sometimes for curiosity's sake. Now I call them out and embarrass them. Hey, it's fun, *and* they are being rude anyway!

Unfortunately these types have infiltrated society at the highest levels. They are everywhere, they have conquered the planet!

Allegedly during wartime conferences, it was Hitler who did all the talking. World leaders do it. It is bad manners and it is just plain bad. These people can obviously be great leaders but they are not great team players.

What we all want to hear, especially the narcissists, is about *ourselves*. We want the other person to show an interest in ourselves and our career. We never want to hear too much about the other person, but this really does depend.

When making a speech in public. It needs to relate to the audience, or they are going to tune out. Everyone has narcissism built in. It's why we have the newer car, the newer phone. But any speech, needs to be about the audience. This applies to all interpersonal communication.

There has got to be a better way!

In setting up a speaking business, myself and Nathan, decided there were better, more effective ways of teaching public speaking.

In particular in terms of overcoming shyness before a crowd. This lets a person's natural charisma come to the fore.

Since we both happen to be fairly decent at holding an audience's attention, we decided to make this into a business.

One thing I personally like to employ while speaking is intuition.

Use your intuition to know when to pause and for other things

The best speakers are going to be using their intuition in a lot of things. Why not in speaking? Your own natural intuition is talking to you all of the time.

It is actually telling you: 'You're talking too much.' Or, 'you're not talking enough, your audience is bored! Your audience is excited.'

But that knowledge is not very useful. You can actually direct your intuition towards it telling you when to pause, and when to keep going.

How? What feels right? Do that. If it feels comfortable to do a pause, to stop, to continue, then do that. If it feels uncomfortable, and you are losing energy, you're doing it wrong.

If your speech is effortless, and you're actually gaining energy while speaking, you're doing it right and your mind is helping you along!

Sometimes it is possible to get so wrapped up in a speech that we don't know when to quit. That's bad. If the audience is bored, change tack.

Stop that topic and go onto the next topic on your list of items which you just *know* is amazing and sensational!

39

Starting and finishing off

You want to finish off a speech the same way it has begun, basically with some kind of impact, some kind of joke. You might therefore like to continue the joke you might have begun at the start.

I always tell people to start with a bang and finish with a bang. Make it along similar lines to bring the speech full circle and the audience will think: 'Oh, but how clever!'

Dale Carnegie

I hope Toastmasters will forgive me for saying this but someone about eighty years ago decided to clone Dale Carnegie's speaking course and call it 'Toastmasters.' That's certainly what it feels like!

I have a collection of Dale Carnegie books. Dale was very active in the early 20th century. He started out giving seminars and workshops on Public Speaking.

His courses were often on other topics such as how to overcome shyness, etc, but he did this by delivering the same public speaking course over and over. This made people more able to overcome nervousness and become more confident in other parts of life.

I have one of his early books, a public speaking course. It is full of ideas and rigid rules on 'how one should behave while speaking.' Little tricks that 'one must do.' I also have a later book, and a much later book, written when he was old.

It seems, as he went along, he he discarded everything he himself had been taught in the early years. He started to realise that the natural authenticity latent in every person is superior, if brought out correctly, to any rigid rule, one might learn in an earlier-style nineteenth-century speaking course.

Everyone is already a fantastic speaker. They haven't realised it yet. They have not flicked the switch. That switch is there, believe me.

I've seen it flick from humble to pro in a matter of weeks. I've watched people have their lives and careers change. I'm not making any of this up. I know because they've told me this.

This is something I try and bring out in my own seminars. We try and bring out the best way that person has, to speak. And tune them individually.

So I encourage you to read one of Dale Carnegie's later books on public speaking. For instance: 'The Quick and Easy way to Effective Speaking.'

Vocal Variety

Vocal variety means you need to vary your tone and pitch. You will find yourself doing this naturally once you speak on a topic that greatly interests you. If you do not do this, people will whisper that you are a cure for insomniacs.

It is not a bad thing if you don't use vocal variety. You're just being you, but *do* try. As I said, a serious person can simply talk about an entertaining topic. This is perfectly reasonable and makes for a fantastic speech.

Remember, speaking is always entertainment, while being vulnerable and keeping it simple, rather than serious sermonising.

Start with a bang, sometimes finish with a bang

Say something dramatic. Say something crazy. One man tried to win a contest by talking about a piercing on his manhood. He did not win but he sure knew how to deliver a good speech!

Ultimately it is all about talking in a reasoned, well mannered tone. If you can do that, it is ok to be a little bit crazy while up on stage.

Being Funny

Being funny is easy. Funny is unexpected. Say unexpected wild things. Start trying this by drawing unexpected conclusions to the audience while talking. People will laugh. Go back to the unexpected conclusion at the end for a perfect ending.

You are always 'being told' the best way. Just listen: Connect to the Universe.

The *Brain is a Radio Transmitter* to all the ideas and wonders of the universe.

When he wrote 'Think and Grow Rich,' Napoleon Hill said that buried in the book is a secret. Once you became aware of the secret, you would potentially become as successful as the great captains of industry, who are supposedly fully aware of it!

I read that book again and again, trying to find the 'secret.' Then I found it! What I realised he was saying is that the brain, as a radio transmitter, actually receives ideas from the universe, when focused upon and with a positive intention mediated by prayer and by other means.

So if you focus on your 'major life purpose' as he called it, you could intuitively call advice from the universe. You could effectively run almost on autopilot!

I began to advise my clients in public speaking on this method. Speak like your hero essentially, and you channel some of their powers! And it works wonders. People go from inert, to 'all guns firing' while up on stage!

I now know that that is only *one* secret in that book. He buried lots of secrets in there and used the 'singular secret' idea as a marketing gimmick.

I know this because he must have seen what I saw: when you run seminars and tell the one secret, only a few in the crowd are impressed or actually believe it is possible.

Different people are going to be impressed by 'different secrets' found in that book. And by hiding the secret, the book could suddenly appeal to everybody.

To Conclude

To conclude, I would like to suggest that you take the advice given by Dale Carnegie all those years ago in his written final works on Public Speaking, in which he threw out the rule books of the previous century.

Be enthusiastic. Be burning with passion. Be sincere and be passionate about what you are talking about.

If a speaker can do this he is immediately the best speaker there is. If a speaker can assume himself a world expert in his field and 'step up' by stepping into the energy of a greater speaker than himself, he will find himself acting in ways he has seen before maybe on television.

He will be surprised to be suddenly acting in these ways, as if he had many years experience in public speaking. I don't know how it works and I know it sounds like a miracle, but it is as true as day follows the night.

Public speaking is easier thank you think!

Thank you for reading.

About Charles and Nathan's Speaking Workshops: *SPEAK WITH EASE*.

At 'Speak with Ease' we offer ***unique*** speaking workshops to take your team to the next level. You deserve the best team you can get, so visit,

www.speakwithease.com.au

Thank you!

About the Author

As a historian, Dr Charles has studied the great historical figures. Charles specialises in teaching Intuition as well as examples of Historical Leadership, in which subjects he runs seminars and workshops. Further information, please see:

www.sensibleeducation.com.au

About Plus Ultra Books

Be sure to check out our other books, online, in Ebook and Paperback format.

Self Help, Mysticism, Ancient Mysteries.

www.plusultrabooks.com.au